owjc

D1187303

SHOCK ZONE™

DEADLY AND DANGEROUS

DEADLY
Adorable
ANIMALS

NADIA HIGGINS

Lerner Publications Company • Minneapolis

Lerner Publications Company
A division of Lerner Publishing Group, Inc.
241 First Avenue North
Minneapolis, MN 55401 U.S.A.

Website address: www.lernerbooks.com

Library of Congress Cataloging-in-Publication Data

Higgins, Nadia.
    Deadly adorable animals / by Nadia Higgins.
        p.   cm. — (Shockzone™—deadly and dangerous)
    Audience: 9–14.
    Includes index.
    ISBN 978–1–4677–0598–1 (lib. bdg. : alk. paper)
        1. Animal defenses—Juvenile literature. 2. Animal chemical
defenses—Juvenile literature. I. Title.
QL759.H44 2013
591.47—dc23   2012015331

Manufactured in the United States of America
1 – PC – 12/31/12

TABLE OF CONTENTS

You know how people gush over an animal just because it's furry or chubby or has giant eyes?

"It's sooooo cute!"
"Don't you just want to take it home?"
"I think it likes me!"

Well, what if that adorable animal could talk? It'd probably say something like, "Feed me!" or "Get off my land!"

'Cause guess what? Nature isn't a Disney movie. **Adorable doesn't mean nice.** And really, that's a good thing. Being nice is kind of a drawback when survival means crushing your dinner's skull with your teeth.

Be careful about aproaching a cute chimpanzee . . . .

What's the coolest way to be deadly? Poison is always a good bet. So are razor-sharp teeth, pointy claws, and punishing hooves. Of course, anything can be deadly if used the right way. Plenty of animals have been known to get nasty with their necks, noses, and elbows.

Why do animals attack? Catching prey is one reason. Protecting territory is another. Males fight for the right to mate with females. And females fight to protect their young. Then there's prey that kills to save its own life. That's always awesome.

But sometimes there seems to be no good reason for a blood fest. As you're about to find out, cute animals can get really ugly.

You could get a face full of pointy teeth looking your way!

GIANT OTTERS

Don't you want to take this guy home and name him "Poopsie"? Now imagine that face sinking its teeth into the side of an anaconda or chewing on the tail of a living crocodile. This cutie-pie would be delighted to partake in either of these activities.

Giant otters are probably the snortiest, squeakiest, and splashiest animals of South America's rivers. At first, they seem like a bunch of rowdy kids in a pool—until they get hungry, which is pretty much always.

When it comes to mauling, thrashing, gnawing, and generally tearing apart other animals, giant otters like to keep it all in the family. They hunt in packs of about eight, and the female is top dog.

Check out the crafty way they have of getting fish:

1. Giant otters all swim to the middle of the river.
2. They take big breaths into their huge lungs. Now they're all set for a nice, long underwater chase.
3. They rip through the water like the swimming machines they are. Their droopy whiskers work like sonar, picking up even the tiniest fish movements.
4. The otters drive the fish to the edges of the water. Then it's bye-bye, fishies. The otters simply scoop their prey right out of the shallow water.

sonar = a device that finds objects underwater by sending out sound waves that are reflected by the objects

To eat, they float on their backs. *Crunch!* They feast on the animals that squirm in their claws.

An otter uses its sharp teeth and powerful jaws to rip into a fish dinner.

Slow Lorises

This furry fella comes from the forests of Southeast Asia. Have you even seen such adorable eyes? Don't you want to tickle his teeny feet? Sounds fun...but that's probably not such a good idea.

Why? The slow loris is venomous. It's the only venomous primate in the world. And guess where it keeps its venom? In handy sacs on the sides of its elbows.

primate = a kind of mammal with feet and hands that can grab things

When another creature starts bugging a slow loris, the loris doesn't run away. It gets very still. If you're lucky, it will hiss a little. That means, "Back off before I lick my elbows and spread venom all over my sharp teeth. I will then sink those teeth into your flesh. This will cause extreme pain and perhaps death."

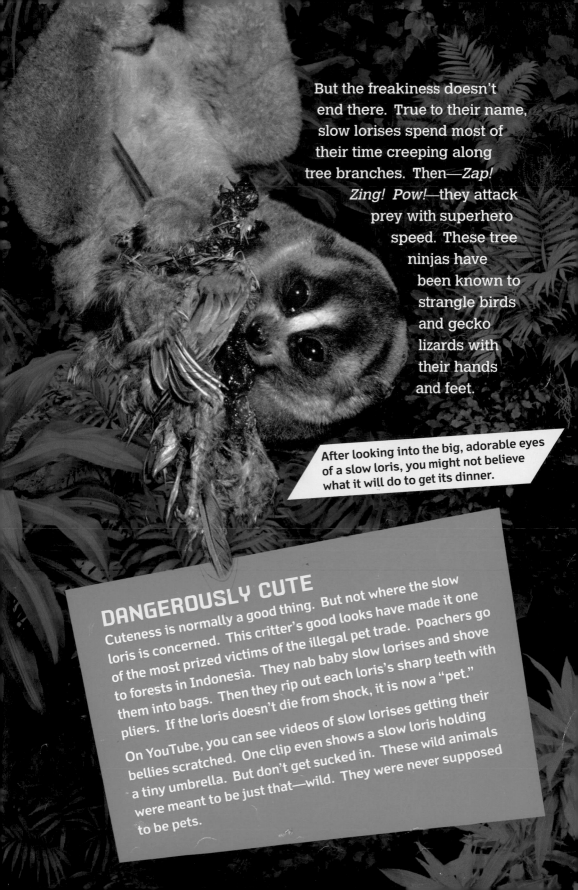

But the freakiness doesn't end there. True to their name, slow lorises spend most of their time creeping along tree branches. Then—*Zap! Zing! Pow!*—they attack prey with superhero speed. These tree ninjas have been known to strangle birds and gecko lizards with their hands and feet.

After looking into the big, adorable eyes of a slow loris, you might not believe what it will do to get its dinner.

DANGEROUSLY CUTE

Cuteness is normally a good thing. But not where the slow loris is concerned. This critter's good looks have made it one of the most prized victims of the illegal pet trade. Poachers go to forests in Indonesia. They nab baby slow lorises and shove them into bags. Then they rip out each loris's sharp teeth with pliers. If the loris doesn't die from shock, it is now a "pet."

On YouTube, you can see videos of slow lorises getting their bellies scratched. One clip even shows a slow loris holding a tiny umbrella. But don't get sucked in. These wild animals were meant to be just that—wild. They were never supposed to be pets.

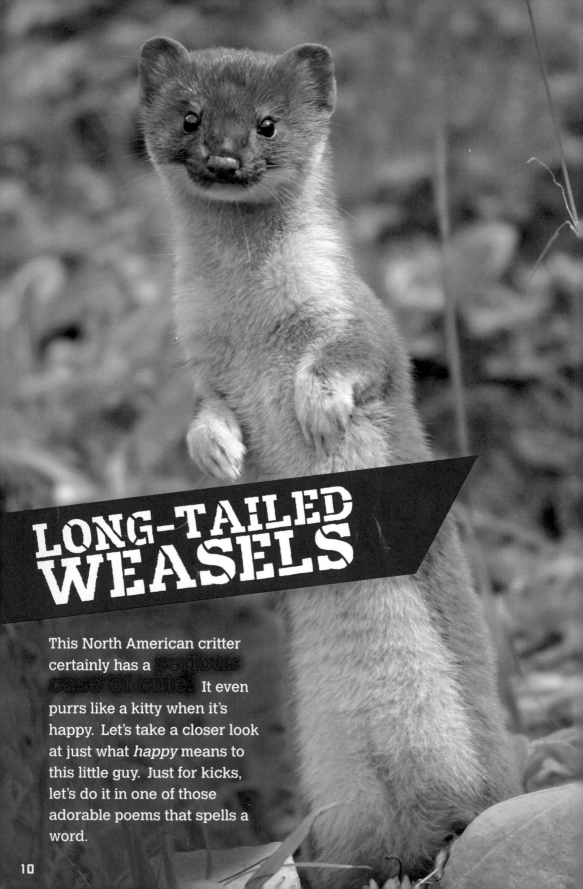

LONG–TAILED WEASELS

This North American critter certainly has a serious case of cute! It even purrs like a kitty when it's happy. Let's take a closer look at just what *happy* means to this little guy. Just for kicks, let's do it in one of those adorable poems that spells a word.

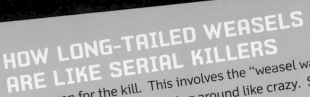

HOW LONG-TAILED WEASELS ARE LIKE SERIAL KILLERS

- They prep for the kill. This involves the "weasel war dance." Basically, this means jumping around like crazy. Somehow, this confuses prey so it won't run away.

- They keep a stash of dead bodies in their burrows. Unlike most animals, weasels kill more than they can eat. When that happens, they drag the dead home, just in case they get the munchies later.

- They do creepy stuff like licking up their victims' blood. They also line their nests with the fur of their prey.

Hungrily devours one-third of its own weight in meat in one day.

Attacks by wrapping its body around its prey.

Plunges its teeth into its victim's skull for a nice, fast kill.

Preys on animals six times its size or more.

Yes, that could include you.

Long-tailed weasels have no qualms about attacking animals much bigger than themselves.

BOTTLENOSE DOLPHINS

Bottlenose dolphins once belonged in the same category as rainbows, sunshine, and love songs. People never had to worry about being shipwrecked because along would come a friendly dolphin to rescue them.

But that was before the porpoise bodies started washing up onshore. Porpoises are basically smaller, dumber versions of dolphins. Starting in the 1990s, their dead, beaten bodies were washing up by the hundreds. At first scientists blamed boat propellers. Then they noticed the teeth marks—marks that perfectly matched up with a bottlenose dolphin's teeth.

This dolphin rams its head into the side of an unsuspecting porpoise.

Here's how it all goes down. Two or three young adult male dolphins will chase down a single porpoise. They'll beat and bite their victim. Often they'll throw it up in the air. The porpoise will twirl so fast that its spine spins faster than the rest of its body. This basically tears up its insides.

In one sick move, the dolphins use their noses to raise the porpoise's tail. That way, the porpoise can't lift its head out of the water to breathe. Once the porpoise dies, the dolphins lose interest and swim away.

Wait—what? That's right. The dolphins don't even eat the porpoise. It's not a territory thing either. And the two species don't compete for prey. Scientists have a bunch of guesses as to why dolphins behave this way. But when it comes right down to it, nobody really knows why they can be such psychos.

A porpoise pokes its head above the water. It should probably be on the lookout for killer dolphins!

Puffer Fish

"Pick me up! Let's be friends!"

If puffer fish could talk, that's what they'd say, right? These guys have got to be the chubbiest, smiliest fish in the sea—until the spikes come out. And then you realize that this fish's "smile" holds teeth that could bite off your finger. And the only reason the fish is so chubby is that it's afraid of you.

Usually, puffer fish look like regular fish with smooth skin and creepy dead eyes. But when they sense danger, they gulp up air or water. Then—poof!—instant spikes. Being prickly and beach-ball shaped keeps them safe from predators, which prefer things that are easier to eat.

See those spikes? Beware! They're part of the puffer fish's defense system.

But say you're *really* craving some puffer fish sushi. In that case, this little fishy has a killer surprise in store for you! Shortly after your meal, your lips may feel a bit tingly. Then come the headache and dizziness. Then pain rips through your stomach...until you can't move a muscle or even breathe.

Puffer fish are one of the most toxic creatures on Earth. Just one fish holds enough poison to kill thirty grown men!

DEADLY DINNER

In Japan, some people consider puffer fish a delicious treat. That's because not every part of the fish is poisonous. Specially trained chefs know just which parts to cut away. Or at least their customers hope they do! A handful of people die every year from eating poorly prepared puffer fish.

HOUSE CATS

Your cat may be the cutest snuggle puss on the planet. But is it also a biological weapon?

Cats are the No. 1 carrier of a parasite called *T. gondii*. In fact, this microscopic bugger can reproduce *only* in a cat's intestines. And the parasite has a crafty way of making sure its species survives. Let's take a look at how *T. gondii's* survival strategy goes down.

parasite = a creature that lives off another living thing, usually harming it in some way

1. A cat poops outside in the dirt. The poop is full of *T. gondii*.
2. Along comes a rat. It eats basically anything it can find. That includes food scraps covered in dirt—the same dirt where the cat did its business. Infected cat poop gets into the rat's food.
3. *T. gondii* goes into the rat's brain.
4. The cat germs *take over* the rat's brain. The rat loses its fear of cats, which means...
5. The rat becomes an easy snack for a cat. The parasites happily land once again inside a cat's intestines. Soon the parasites are pooped out, and the cycle begins again.

This microscopic image shows *T. gondii*—the killer in kitty poop.

That's freaky. But what does that have to do with people? THIS: As of 2012, more than 60 million Americans were infected with *T. gondii*. For most, that means maybe a sore throat for a week or two. But could there be more? After all, the parasite can turn a rat into suicidal cat bait. What does it do to human brains?

Scientists are beginning to believe that *T. gondii* DOES mess with how people react to danger. One study showed that infected people were two and half times more likely to be in a traffic accident than other people.

What does it all mean? Basically that yes, kitty poop can kill.

GOLDEN POISON DART FROGS

This hoppy little critter is just soooo little. And shiny. And really and truly golden. Even if you're not two years old, you just can't help reaching out to touch. Which is why, the next time you're in the rain forests of Colombia, you should do yourself a favor and wear handcuffs.

Even touching a golden poison dart frog could mean fast and painful death. This guy's skin holds the most powerful poison in nature. The frog's freakishly bright color advertises that fact to bigger creatures, which wisely stay away.

POISON-MAKING MACHINES

This deadly frog doesn't actually come with poison included. Scientists believe the frog's body makes the poison from the bugs it eats. Pet dart frogs that don't eat rain forest bugs aren't poisonous at all.

Native people in Colombia have known about this golden blob of terror for centuries. In fact, hunters once wiped their spears, also known as darts, on the frog. That made the hunters' weapons extra deadly. It's also how the frog got its name.

A native man from Colombia uses a blow gun to kill prey in the rain forest.

Polar Bears

Ice Bear. Lord of the Arctic. God's Dog.

Those are all real nicknames that northern cultures have used for the polar bear. And no wonder. This magnificent creature is the baddest bear out there.

Check it out:

- The polar bear is the world's largest land predator. It weighs in at 1,200 pounds (544 kilograms) or more.
- This guy can't even feel cold unless temps dip below –34°F (–36.7°C).
- A polar bear can sniff out its prey from *20 miles* (32 kilometers) away.

Polar bears mostly eat ringed seals, which are mammals. Even though they live in water, the seals have to come up for air. So they make a bunch of breathing holes in the arctic ice.

A polar bear will wait for days by a breathing hole. It stands there on all fours, totally silent. When the seal comes up—*BAM!* The bear grabs the seal in its 2-inch (5-centimeter) claws. It drags the seal onto the ice. Then it crushes the seal's skull with its teeth.

A polar bear waits at a seal breathing hole *(above)*. When the seal shows itself, the bear grabs for its meal *(left)*.

MAKE 'EM BEG

Once in a while, a polar bear will take down some huge animal, like a walrus. That means leftovers. In that case, a polar bear will share with other polar bears. But only if they beg first. They have to stay low and circle around the bear in charge. Then they meekly touch the boss bear's nose with their own.

PLATYPUSES

This adorable critter from Australia gets a lot of press for being odd. It's furry but has webbed feet and a bill like a duck. It's a mammal that lays eggs. So yes, it's weird, but *deadly*?

Doesn't a platypus basically eat worms? It doesn't even have teeth, right? How deadly can it be?

Very. Just check out the dead dogs and cats that have been killed by platypus venom. Or the guy whose arm swelled up for weeks after a platypus sting.

That's right. Male platypuses have sharp stingers on their heels. They use those stingers to shoot venom into their enemies. And a male platypus's No. 1 enemy? Another male platypus.

Notice how we didn't mention female platypuses just now? That's because they don't have stingers. The main purpose of these heel daggers is to dominate another male. Platypus combat is way fiercer than any UFC match. And the prize? The right to mate with a female.

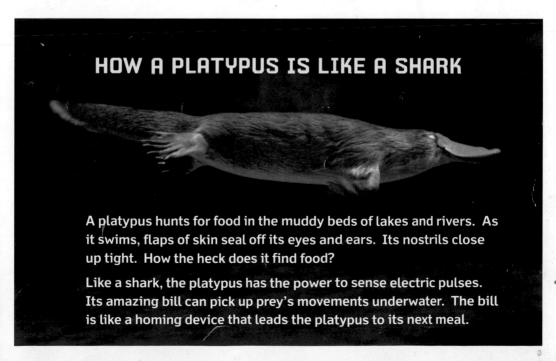

HOW A PLATYPUS IS LIKE A SHARK

A platypus hunts for food in the muddy beds of lakes and rivers. As it swims, flaps of skin seal off its eyes and ears. Its nostrils close up tight. How the heck does it find food?

Like a shark, the platypus has the power to sense electric pulses. Its amazing bill can pick up prey's movements underwater. The bill is like a homing device that leads the platypus to its next meal.

Giraffes

"No!" you gasp. "Giraffes—deadly? That can't be!"

In a way, you're right. Giraffes do spend something like 99 percent of their time chewing leaves and blinking their incredibly long eyelashes. But take a closer look, and you'll discover that a giraffe's life pretty much sucks. They're constantly worried about getting attacked.

It's for that reason that giraffes live in herds and stay away from trees (which are good for hiding predators). It's also why giraffes almost never sit down and sleep only twenty minutes a day (still standing up). Giraffes can't even take a drink for more than a few seconds because that means dropping their heads and letting down their guard.

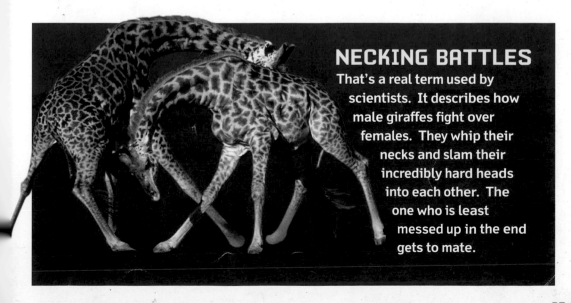

Giraffes take a giant risk when they bend down to get a drink of water. Predators, such as the lioness *(left)*, are lurking everywhere.

Most of all, giraffes never leave their babies—called calves—without a babysitter. *Yet 50 to 70 percent of giraffe calves are killed by predators in their first few months of life.*

Can you blame a giraffe for going a little crazy? After all, sometimes, when a lion comes nipping at your tail, you don't want to run away. You want to use your incredibly powerful legs and sharp hooves. *WHACK!* You want to crush that lion's skull with a single blow—because you can. And because that's how deadly is done, giraffe style.

NECKING BATTLES

That's a real term used by scientists. It describes how male giraffes fight over females. They whip their necks and slam their incredibly hard heads into each other. The one who is least messed up in the end gets to mate.

CHIMPS

Chimpanzees share 98 percent of human DNA. They're furrier, cuter versions of first graders, basically... well, brain-eating first graders with razor-sharp teeth and superhuman strength, that is.

DNA = a substance that stores genetic information. It's carried in every cell of your body. The way your DNA is organized determines tons of stuff about your body and how it works.

Most of the time, a chimp is fine with eating fruit and munching on leaves. But sometimes a chimp gets a hankering for some monkey blood. In that case, it may:

• grab a monkey and bite into its brain;
• wring the monkey's neck with its freakishly strong hands;
• grab the monkey by its legs and slam its head against a tree.

Chimps in motion amid a feeding frenzy tear into a monkey's flesh.

The chimp begins its meal with its favorite part—the monkey's brains. To get at the brains, the chimp tears off the monkey's head. Or it pries open the monkey's skull with its teeth and fingers, the way you might open the top of a banana. The chimp licks the inside of the skull clean. Then it goes on to finish the rest—hair, bones, and all.

HOW TO SURVIVE A CHIMP ATTACK

Chimps have been known to attack and even kill humans. The next time you stumble into chimp territory, remember these tips.

• Don't run! That's like asking a chimp to chase you.

• Instead, hunch down, look down, keep your mouth closed, and quietly back away. That shows you're not looking for a fight.

• If that doesn't work, curl up in a ball. Hopefully, the chimp will lose interest.

• Is there a lake right there? You could jump in that, as chimps can't swim. DON'T climb a tree—obviously!

SWANS

Did you know that most swans mate for life? And they really do touch bills and "kiss"? Plus, their long necks really do make a heart shape!

These are some beautiful animals. You can barely watch one go by without imagining classical music playing in the background—unless, of course, the swan starts beating you with the bony knobs on its huge wings, breaking your arm (yikes!). In that case, the classical music turns to squeaky violins mixed with screams.

Yet let's be fair to swans. The only reason they attack is because you're invading their territory. Swans are some of the most devoted parents in the animal world. They don't know that you're just

trying to take a picture of water lilies to send to your aunt Penelope. When they hiss and bark at you like rabid dogs, that's just their way of saying, "Don't mess with my family!"

They probably won't chase you far. However, when you leave, they just might celebrate with a special victory dance. The swan parents face each other with raised wings. Their calls ring out across the lake. That's their way of saying "Woot! Woot!" in swan talk.

Be careful when out canoeing. You could become the subject of *When Swans Attack!*

FURTHER INFORMATION

Animal Planet: How to Survive an Animal Attack
http://animals.howstuffworks.com/animal-facts/5-animal-attack-videos4.htm
Despite its name, this video really only shows how to survive an attack from a bear or a cougar. Still, the tips here may surprise you (and save your life).

Brownlee, Christen. *Cute, Furry, and Deadly: Diseases You Can Catch from Your Pet!* New York: Franklin Watts, 2008. Consider this your one-stop guide to zoonotic diseases (those passed on from animals to humans). This fun, fact-packed title offers quizzes, interviews with experts, and three true-life case files.

Discovery Channel Survival Videos
http://dsc.discovery.com/videos/survival-videos
Editors at the Discovery Channel have posted their best videos of how people survive in extreme conditions. Learn how to make it through a sandstorm (hint: don't run). See firsthand how one man fends off sunstroke using his own pee. Check out what nasty stuff can count as food. This is one of the grossest sites on the Web.

Doeden, Matt. *Deadly Venomous Animals.* Minneapolis: Lerner Publications Company, 2013. If you loved reading about the animal world's deadliest cuties, you'll also adore this title on deadly venomous critters.

Farris, Melissa. *Deadly Instinct.* Washington, DC: National Geographic, 2011. Looking for action-packed photos of deadly animals fighting to the death? This gorgeous collection of photographs certainly offers that. It also explains why animals attack. Killing prey is just one reason among many.

Guinness World Records
http://www.guinnessworldrecords.com
Read about animal world records you never even thought about, like "loudest purr" or "biggest egg." While you're there, check out weird records like "heaviest weight lifted by tongue." Think you can set a new record? The site tells you how to start.

Leigh, Autumn. *Deadly Pufferfish.* New York: Gareth Stevens, 2011. Learn more about these freaky poisonous fish.

National Geographic Kids' **Page**
http://kids.nationalgeographic.com/kids
Here you can find the latest news about animals as well as games. But the best part of this site is the awesome videos. Click on the heading Creepy to learn about "snail zombies," jumping spiders, and other freaky creatures.

National Wildlife Federation Kids' Page
http://www.nwf.org/Kids.aspx
This site is packed with animal info. You can search by species or just browse. It also offers tons of fun extras, such as games, jokes, and contests. Click on "Outdoor Fun" for step-by-step instructions on how to build a frog pond and other cool projects to get your hands dirty.

Science Channel's Top Ten Library
http://science.discovery.com/top-ten/top-ten.html
Ever wonder what the top ten toxic plants are? What about weirdest sea creatures, giant bugs, or useless body parts? Check out this site for weirdest top ten lists out there.

INDEX

LERNER
SOURCE

Expand learning beyond the printed book. Download free, complementary educational resources for this book from our website, www.lerneresource.com.

The images in this book are used with the permission of: © Michael Poliza/ National Geographic/Getty Images, p. 4; © Simon De Glanville/Alamy, p. 5; © Nicole Duplaix/National Geographic/Getty Images, p. 6; © Christophe Courteau/Minden Pictures, p. 7; © Thomas Marent/Minden Pictures, p. 8; © Biosphoto/Daniel Heuclin, p. 9; © iStockphoto.com/Eva Serrabassa (leaf background); © Ken Hoehn/Papilio/Alamy, p. 10; © Blackpool College/ Oxford Scientific/Getty Images, p. 11; © art-design-photography.com/ flickr/Getty Images, p. 12; Mark Cotter/sZuma Press/Newscom, p. 13 (top); © Bernd Lammel/STERN/Black Star/Newscom, p. 13 (bottom); © Richard Carey/Dreamstime.com, p. 14; © LWA/Photodisc/Getty Images, p. 15 (top); © Yoshikazu Tsuno/AFP/Getty Images, p. 15 (bottom); © Miroslava Kopecka/Dreamstime.com, p. 16; © Dr. Arthur Siegelman/Visuals Unlimited/ CORBIS, p. 17 (top); © Eti Swinford/Dreamstime.com, p. 17 (bottom); © David & Micha Sheldon/F1online/Getty Images, p. 18; © Dietmar Heinz/ Picture Press/Alamy, p. 19 (top); © Mark Moffett/Minden Pictures/CORBIS, p. 19; © Wayne Lynch/All Canada Photos/Getty Images, p. 20; © Wayne Lynch/All Canada Photos/CORBIS, pp. 20–21; © Fred Bruemmer/Peter Arnold/Getty Images, p. 21 (top); © Vladimir Melnik/Dreamstime.com, p. 21 (bottom); © David Watts/Visuals Unlimited/CORBIS, p. 22; © Jean Paul Ferrero/Auscape/Minden Pictures/CORBIS, p. 23 (top); © Rob Griffith/AP/ CORBIS, p. 23 (bottom); © ZSSD/Minden Pictures, p. 24; © iStockphoto. com/Frans Dekkers, p. 25 (top); © Terry Andrewartha/Minden Pictures, p. 25 (bottom); © NHPA/SuperStock, pp. 26, 27 (top); © Duncan Noakes/ Dreamstime.com, p. 27 (bottom); © Brent Black/Perspectives/Getty Images, p. 28; © iStockphoto.com/Elena Elisseeva, p. 29 (top); © Andrew Forsyth/ Minden Pictures, p. 29 (bottom).

Front cover: © Jeff Foott/Discovery Channel Images/Getty Images.

Main body text set in Calvert MT Std Regular 11/16.
Typeface provided by Monotype Typography.